NO LONGER PROPERTY OF
SEATTLE PUBLIC LIBRARY RECEIVED

NOV 3 0 2019

BROADVIEW LIBRAR

YOU CAN'T KILL ME TWICE

(so please treat me right)

Charlyne Yi

Andrews McMeel
PUBLISHING®

NO LONGER PROPERTY OF
SEATTLE PUBLIC LIBRARY

Dedicated to the city of Flint

You Can't Kill Me Twice copyright © 2019 by Charlyne Yi.
All rights reserved. Printed in the United States of America.
No part of this book may be used or reproduced in any
manner whatsoever without written permission except
in the case of reprints in the context of reviews.

Andrews McMeel Publishing
a division of Andrews McMeel Universal
1130 Walnut Street, Kansas City, Missouri 64106

www.andrewsmcmeel.com

19 20 21 22 23 BVG 10 9 8 7 6 5 4 3 2 1

ISBN: 978-1-5248-5075-3

Library of Congress Control Number: 2019944759

Editor: Allison Adler
Art Director: Diane Marsh
Production Editor: Dave Shaw
Production Manager: Carol Coe

ATTENTION: SCHOOLS AND BUSINESSES
Andrews McMeel books are available at quantity discounts
with bulk purchase for educational, business, or sales
promotional use. For information, please e-mail the
Andrews McMeel Publishing Special Sales Department:
specialsales@amuniversal.com.

I don't judge a book by its cover;
I judge it by its spine.

I am undressing you in my mind,
to dress you up right:

    in thermals, a coat, scarf, toque,
    wool socks, and boots.

It's cold out and I care about you.
Sometimes, tenderness is sexy.

I am a witch,
a vulnerable, vulgar woman,
made of exquisite light, tap-dancing mice
who wear top hats, and eat fire.

I prefer to use my magic for good,
but if you hurt me, I swear to God
I'll turn you inside out
like a human pocket of flesh
that will never hold anything again.

Is there any evidence that this is love?

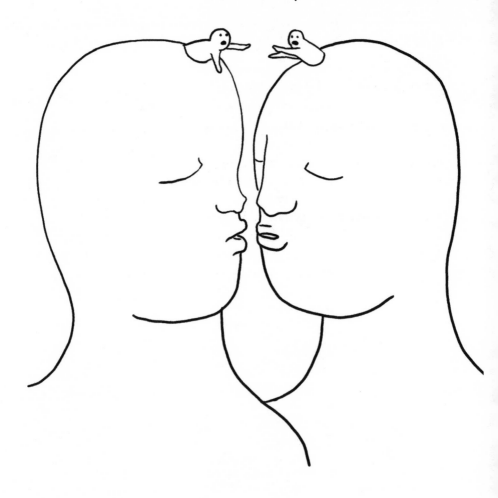

What I
Ate Today

FOR BREAKFAST: I ate two sunrises (over easy), two
scrambled universes, and two days' worth of nostalgia.

FOR LUNCH: I ate seven secrets, a carousel of memories,
several hundred forgotten dreams, and a popular song
that everyone was sick of hearing.

FOR DINNER: I ate the mistakes made by a man who could never
forgive himself but really should, twenty-three almost-sneezes
that haunted your nose, and an entire roll of kodachrome, so that
I have colorful memories for when I am old.

It would come to no one's surprise that I have gas.

I'm not afraid to die. I'm afraid of being dead while I'm alive.

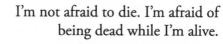

I threw my goddamn emotional baggage
off the docks and into the ocean
and the goddamn sonuvabitch popped up floating!
Who on God's green earth taught it to swim?

My partner reads the newspaper
first because I always wet it
with my tears.

Just kidding,
I don't have a partner
but I'm slowly building one out of
papier-mâché.

Action Hero

When I became single,
I tried to jump into sex
like an action hero,
trying to break through the glass
but doing it all wrong—
bumping my head into the window,
accidentally losing my balance,
falling through it,
and finally toppling over
onto the ground
naked beside glass,
sparkling and sharp,
afraid to look
into the eyes of a stranger,
as I tuck away my sad,
and pretend to be tough
like Bruce Willis.

There's a cat who hops
from rooftop to rooftop.
And when our eyes have closed shop,
he whispers things we want to hear, like,
"I love you, Ethel, your existence is not meaningless.
Let's get fucking weird together
and drink each other's tears, Ethel."

He's a liar,
but he's also a good friend.

When I moved, I gave away everything
that reminded me of you, even our blanket.
If it was cold, I slept under a pile of coats.
I pushed all the furniture (that was a two-person job)
down the stairs by myself. All the neighbors
thought they were watching a Laurel and Hardy film
with just Hardy. I'm glad they got a good laugh
as I slid down the stairs with that big oak desk.

When we got these pieces, you told me
I'd never have to worry about carrying the load by myself.
That was a good joke.

Patience is not my strong suit,
but I'm trying to wear it casually with jeans.

I can't read people;
I'm illiterate.

THE STUDY OF TYPES OF LOVE OF FRIENDSHIP, FAMILY & ROMANCE

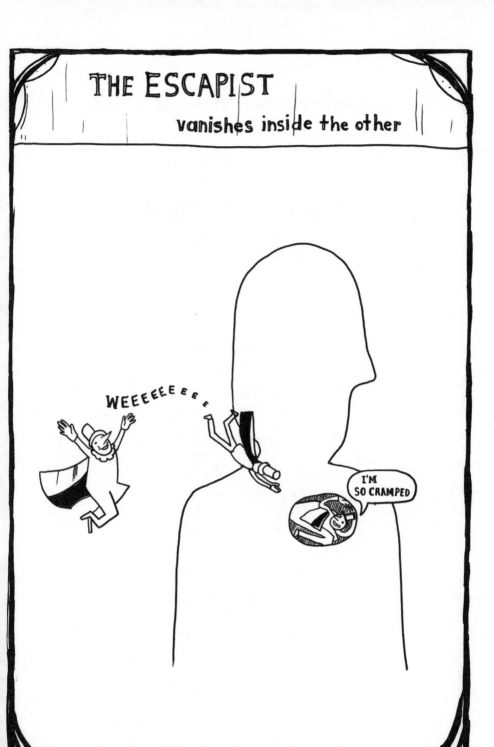

THE CONQUEROR
& DESTROYER

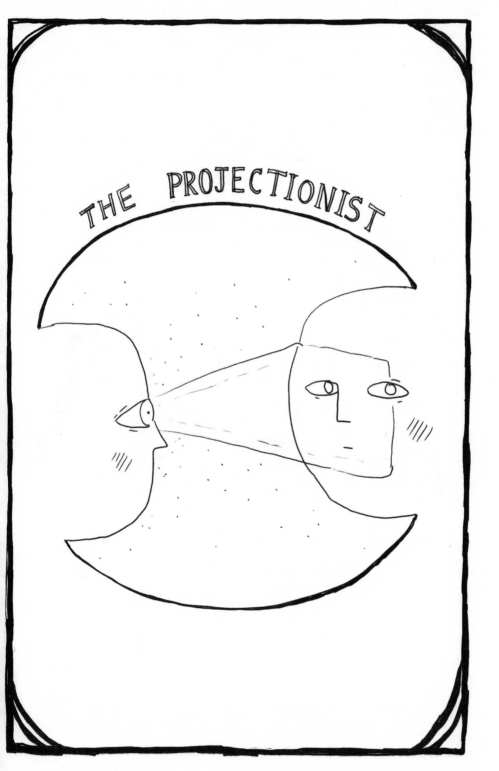

THE PROJECTIONIST

THE BALANCING ACT

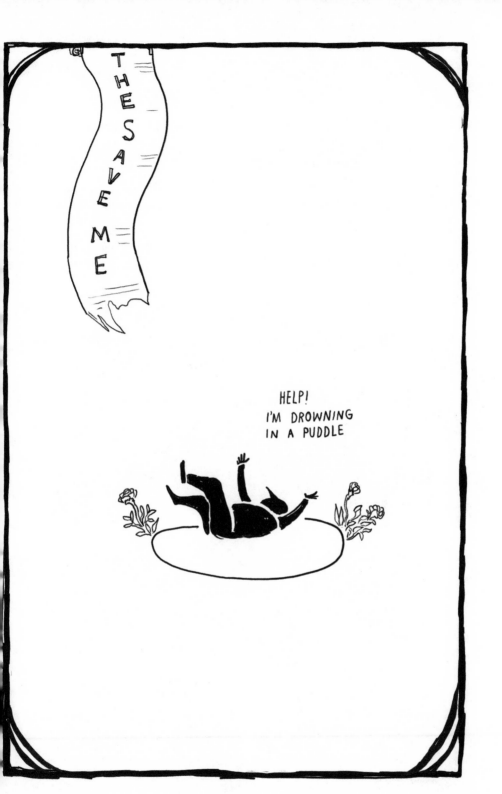

THE COEXISTERS

You say so much, that you love butterflies.
There are at least thirty-eight of them pinned to your wall.
                              Please do not tell me you
                              love me next.

The streets are crumbling,
peeling like an old scab,
and every time I see a plant
break through the cracks,
I think, "Fuck yeah,
nature's striking back!"

I was born from the Devil,
crawled out of her hellhole
when she was sleeping to her favorite sitcom,
cut my umbilical with just my gums,
and headed straight for California.

It's 5:47 p.m.
and I am drunk in Signal Hill.
Oil drills are drilling into the darkness
and in this bar, there are six bikers next to me,
verbally beating each other like piñatas.

(I pick up one of the candies off the ground
when nobody is looking. It tastes okay.)

A child bangs his head
against a wall,
trying to understand
why the adults supervising this world
need convincing that his father
shouldn't be murdered because of his black skin.

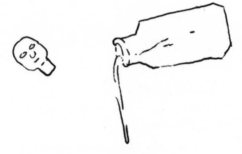

Bodies should not be emptied so casually of their life.

There's an angry Bukowski
trapped inside this tiny Asian woman's body
and no one takes him seriously
as he kicks and hollers,
"Get away from my time machine, you whores!"
sitting alone in the photo booth.
The photos come out, and he wonders
who that Asian woman is.

He said that I am his worst nightmare: a woman.

At night, I drown Bluebird Bukowski
in love and kindness as he cries to the voice
of his mother.

TABLE

Romance is no longer on the table.
in fact,
there is no table.

There are, however, two chairs
facing opposite ways,
if you'd like to have a conversation sometime
to see if we can listen
and give and take
words
and bridge minds,
to see if we can eventually
turn our chairs around,
eat off cafeteria trays,
and see if we can see
eye to eye.

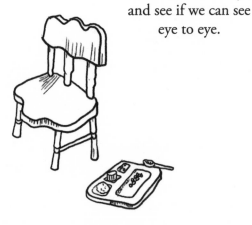

I strangled my ego
till it could not breathe.
I strangled my ego
till there was nothing left
but me.

—what'd you do last night?

When words fly, winged and vulnerable
from the depths of their hell,
maybe then you can hear their song,
it's a tragic but hilarious melody
full of optimism,
it's unusual and true,
it's their soul,
like a magnet,
pulling on you.

I cried at your wedding
because you married someone terrible.

I think it'd be a good idea if the KKK used plastic bags as masks instead.

There's an unwritten, unwelcomed bible that says,
"Just don't be a fucking asshole."

I planted a row
of spines
in case
anyone
needs one.

How will anyone be racist
when they are ghosts and have no skin?

Dear Dad,

You're a coward.

Signed,
A Stranger

The humans stared at their screens
as they missed another sunset.
Too bad it was the last.

Complacency killed the humans.
Curiosity led the cats into a peaceful
existence in which they prospered
and learned from the cats
that died before them.

"Please don't die."
Earth: "I'll try my best."

The Optometrist

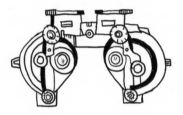

Which lens looks better?

REPRESSION

DEPRESSION

REALITY

Only seeing the bad is *depression.*
Only seeing the good is *repression.*

But to see both the darkness and light
is reality. To see what's at stake
is what makes the world
so humble and beautiful.

I placed an egg under you
to see if you could hatch it
but your butt swallowed it up.

Get out of your head.

I feel guilty eating raisins
because it's like
they're the senior citizens
of grapes.

I saw a billboard that asked me
if I wanted to go to Hell.

When I called the number,
I told them I was interested
but they only offered ways to go to Heaven,
which is very misleading.

Babies don't have a poker face.

In a single minute they've
exploded in laughter,
shat themselves,
wailed screeches of hunger
interluded with quiet confusion,
and found solace
in being held,
which was met with violent rupture
from the annoyance
of being held.

I wonder at what age we train our faces to lie.

He came back to his desk
with ants all over.
He smashed the army,
lifting them of their souls,
sending their bodies
deep into the lined paper.
Their mangled legs
strayed from their heads,
looked like music notes,
which completed his opera.

I bought two large ice bags
and plopped them into my bed
because I missed the cold touch of a man.

When I woke up, he was gone
and my bed was wet.

Typical man.

when you kissed me,
you slipped some food into my mouth.
do i look like a baby bird?
       never mind,
       don't answer that.

Charlyne Yi

Anytime a bunch of guys are bragging about
the size of their penises, I like to imagine a day
where they're bragging about the size of their
hearts and how well they loved.

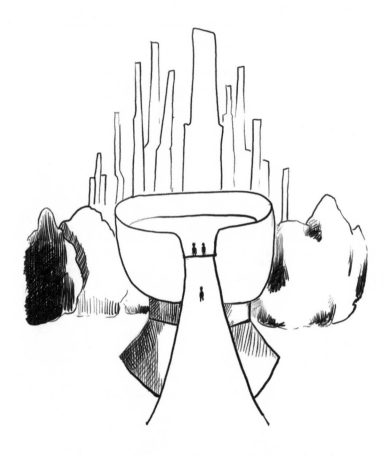

The humans all gathered around the giant bowl
and stared at God's stool because they were gross.

I don't have any tattoos
because I'm afraid of pain
and commitment.

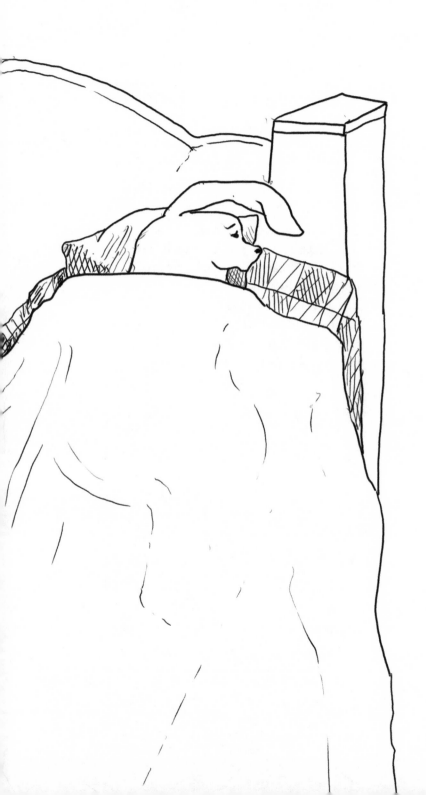

I don't want any ordinary love.
I am particles carried in old music boxes
with songs you can only hear in dreams,
and if you are to walk with me,
you have thunder in your chest,
starlight in your speech,
and you must raise your fist
and shatter the roof of reality with me.

THE SCIENCE OF PRESSURE

There is so much pressure
all around you
that it's condensed
your molecules, pushing you
deeper into yourself,
compressing you
into a hardened person.

I'd rather buy a book than a bra.
I'd rather paint a hundred watercolors,
build twenty-eight automatons,
roll around in dirt,
secretly make oatmeal every day in motels,
catch a rare meteor shower on the hood of my car,
pee in the woods, fix an old flute,
talk to a wise spider,
walk ten miles with an old friend,
and plant carrots and beets
(waiting patiently for them to grow to eat),
than shave my legs, pits, or buy a bra.
Dear god, there are so many
beautiful, amazing things I'd rather do!

The Toronto Airport

I saw the Dalai Lama
riding on the back of a golf cart
to get to his gate in time.

Several teenagers got up around me
and stampeded after him, taking photos.

"I don't know who the Dolly Llama is,
but I know he's famous."

(I could tell from the way she said it,
it was spelled wrong.)

"That's a good photo of you and Dolly."

"Thanks. You know why all the women
on covers of magazines look beautiful?
They use a computer program called Photoshop
to make their faces look better. I'm going to use it to
get rid of all my flaws like my wrinkles and
freckles."

I drove past a Beauty School, stopped in.
They were holding telescopes to each other's eyes,
making each other's souls bright and full of magic.
They talked about the world, dreams, and their hearts.

It was truly a school of beauty.

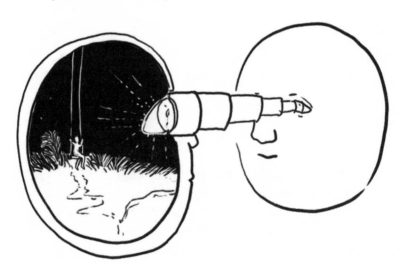

How many inches off the ground
till it's considered sky?

I made a wish I could hold your face just once.

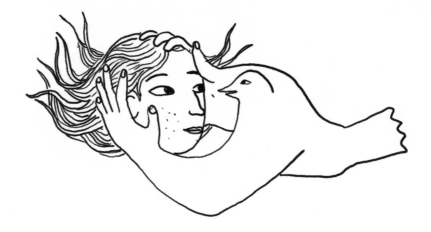

Do you love me less now that you have me?

Yes.

No one can take that much hot and cold.
It'll break anyone. This isn't based on psychology,
it's just physics.

—Studies on romance, climate change, and the effects of alternating
extreme temperatures on glass.

There are two glasses that are half-empty,
that think they can complete each other.

But every time they go into each other's glasses,
they lose themselves completely.

That's the catch: You can't be anyone else's half.

You need to fill yourself up, so you can be two glasses
clinking and toasting, enjoying one another.

My first car was a rough relationship.

First it started to smoke,
then it started to drink,
and then it died.

She was embarrassed
her life was receding
like a hairline.

But neither her life ending
nor going bald
was a thing to be ashamed of.

When she left her body,
her hair continued
to grow.

the story of THE BACKPEDALING MAN:

> Well, he was quite afraid to get hurt
> so he moved backward when forward.
> He said, "I love you,
> I can't love you."
>
> He said, "I am here for you,
> but I've already left town."
>
> He hugs you a hello, which is really a goodbye,
> unless you say goodbye first then he's likely
> to stick around.
>
> So I ask you, "Sir Backpedaling Man,
> what makes you happy?"
> He sits down, puts his lips
> to his steaming cup of soup,
> and in a low sturdy voice says,
> "If I could just sit down
> and take in
> you, me, and
> those particles ballroom dancing around us
> . . . if I wasn't so scared, I would be happy.
> But I'm afraid of missing you and the memories
> we could've shared."

Charlyne Yi

You lit your cigarette
but the light behind your eyes went out.
        My dear, what are we to do with you?

dear mental illness,

why did you take so many people i love away?

brokenhearted,
me

I buttoned up my chest—
too much heart cleavage
was showing.

I woke up,
got in my car, and drove.

Like a Ouija board,
something was pulling me.
I drove through the night into the other side.
Somehow, I'm in Salem now,
and it's sunrise.

I'm playing a rickety flute,
held together by old cobwebs.
Notes hang in the air,
legs dangle from the docks,
and my insides crash like the waters around me
as I think of the women
who were hanged here.

I walk to the Witch Museum,
and a sly seventy-eight-year-old crone guides us.
She asks the room of collected strangers
to consider the origins of Witch Hunts.

She stands proudly and explains,

When there is pain, people want a scapegoat,
and those in power blame those on the fringes.
They blame the outsiders.
With Pearl Harbor, they blamed the Japanese Americans.
With AIDS, they blamed the gay communities.

And now that you have some examples,
here's a hardball for you:
Terrorism. Do you think Muslims are to blame?

The silence was fat.

The answer is no!
Goddammit, weren't you listening?
We need to stop passing down pain.
We need to learn from our history,
educate our children's hearts,
and do better.

Now get the hell out of here!

She winked, propped the door open,
and had a sparkle in her eyes that most people didn't.
Her eyes weren't glazed over,
she was sharp, full of fire,
and, holy shit,
she was alive.

Dreams disguised as memories,
dressed in coats
of humanlike skin.

I miss all the things I can't remember.

So often we are unconsciously
with romantic partners who are
like our parents—we want to prove
that if we could change our partner,
that our parents can change too
and can love us.

But the trick is: Our parents do love us.
It's just that they have a real fucked-up way
of showing it.

White powerful men
want to reappropriate
the term "Witch Hunt"
when defending themselves
from being held accountable for
sexually harassing,
raping,
and gaslighting
women
when the origins derive
from the abuse of women.
Literally beating them,
hanging them,
and burning them
to death.

Stop pouring breath
into the mouths
of the monsters
we won't let die.

Charlyne Yi

When I was eighteen,
my father told me not to smoke cigarettes;
he had a dream that shook him:
I had died of lung cancer.

When I was twenty-one,
I found out that my dad was a pedophile.
He and my oldest sister told me if I told anyone,
my mom would commit suicide,
that I was selfish, evil,
and a piece of shit.

I told my dad that he was my cancer and that I was dying
because of him. I begged him to tell the truth and set me free.
But he wanted me to die.

The Death of the Comedian

She didn't feel very funny
after he stabbed her belly button
and filled his tin cup
with her light.

"This tastes
SOOOO GOOD!"

When he was done,
he wiped his mouth,
pulled out a wine cork,
and with his dirty, fat fingers,
plugged the place where her
umbilical once was.

He walked over her body,
"Life . . . ," he laughed to himself,
shook his head,
walked onto the stage,
and told his first joke.

Reality took off his top hat
and realized he was going bald.

My heart's been avalanched,
torched, hanged, shot twenty-eight times by a shotgun;
and still I love.

I saw a homeless man saying,
        "Hi, hello, hi, hello."
But people passed, never daring to make
eye contact or throw a hello back.

I said to him,
        "Hello, how are you?"
And he said, "Oh, thank god! I was beginning
to believe I didn't exist or that I had lost my
fucking mind."

Two friends walking
with pockets full of curiosity.

It's night but you can see their souls
ricocheting, staggering,
wild dancing light,
for their hearts are strong enough
to summon a storm.

There are people who talk to you
like you are a mirror.

There are people who talk to you,
projecting old reels of their past onto your face.

And there are some people who can see you, and
suddenly, you don't feel so much like a ghost
anymore.

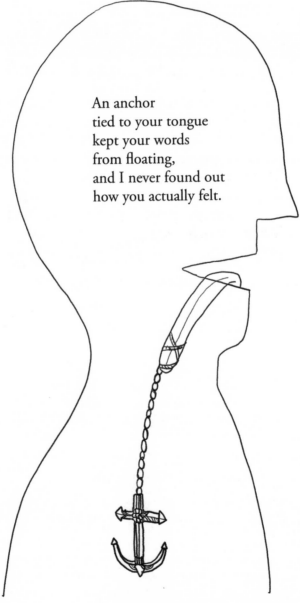

An anchor
tied to your tongue
kept your words
from floating,
and I never found out
how you actually felt.

Charlyne Yi

for my mom

You were born with a pebble for a heart.
You threw your pebble-heart at strangers,
hitting them, hurting them, wondering why
they would not keep your rock for you.
You were born with a pebble for a heart
and you threw it, and it skipped across the lake
that reflected the sky and landed on the moon.

"I have grown out of ways to reach you,"
said the child to the adult
who forgot how to love.

WWII
Manila, Philippines

My grandpa watched his father
get buried alive by the Japanese.
Psychiatric casualties tied to this event
were passed down directly.

My grandpa had PTSD, raised my mom
with untended wounds, had constant flashbacks,
and tried to drown her as a child
in a bucket of water.

My mom raised me, had PTSD,
and I watched her mind collapse,
saw her buried alive, and
every night, she drowned me in threats
of suicide to which I prayed, crying to God
(which sounded more like begging
at the age of three).

One day, she took twenty-two pills,
left a suicide notebook
dedicated to blaming me,
and a photograph of her father.

There's chaos in my heart
and a dream blown in its head,
the idiots will praise destruction
as a cigarette lies down to rest.
A choir is breathing falling notes,
swallowed by my burning dress,
while children play jump rope,
strings anchored
by my sunken head.

Sometimes
holidays make you feel
alone even though
you're not, and so often
you are and you feel fine.

A blizzard takes over New York,
and millions of falling doves
give static to this image.
In the distance,
a golden cab glows
like a treasure,
windows foggy
from a pizza box
shared between a cabbie
and his wife.

The War That Never Was

Two men meet in the middle of the sky
to start a war.

Their men wait
for their command.

After circling each other,
minds doing figure eights,
they decide to fly on top of the tallest mountain
to gain perspective.

On the mountain,
the two drink tea in silence.
They share photos of their families
and watch the tiny villagers below
move about their lives.

They come upon agreement
that they can share the earth,
and there really wasn't ever a good reason to kill.

And no war happened
ever again.

The Dance

The closer we got

the less safe we felt.

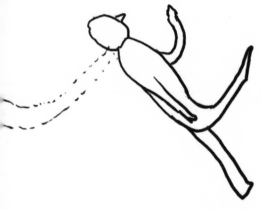

Charlyne Yi

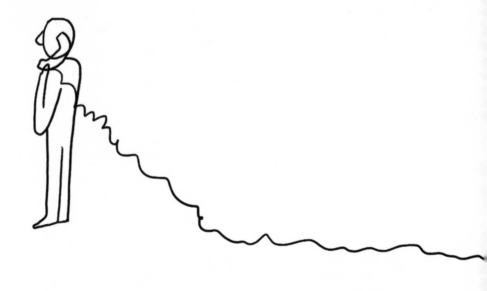

The further we were

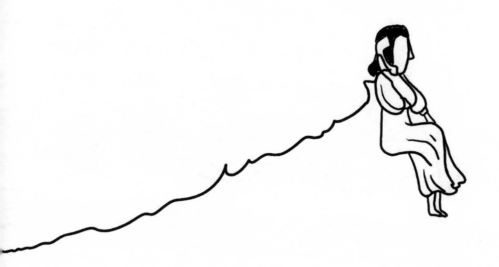

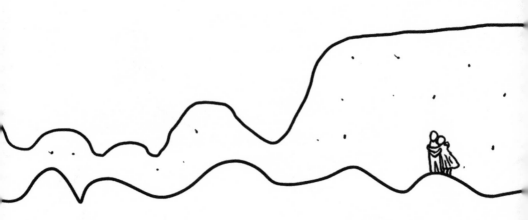

the more tunnels we built.

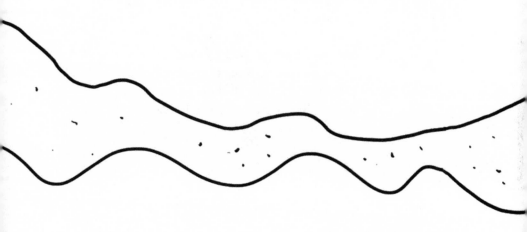

The sunset is hot-pink
like an SOS flare,
as we carve wood into wolves
on our porch.
Our hair has turned gray,
but our voices are still young,
so we do fake "old people's voices"
because even after all these years,
we still like to make each other laugh.

We time travel emotionally
to our past, or anxiously forward
to the future. But if we are not here,
we are deteriorating,
as we cannot be
in two places at once.

Life only lasts a little while,
and if you're lucky, if you're really lucky,
you get to spend it with some pretty special people,
even if they come and go, even if
you drift and grow,
far and stranger
to those who were once close
because life only lasts such a little while.

Two quarrelers
meet in the middle of a dream
and take ten paces.

One shoots in the air,
and the other reacts in fear.

Silence crescendos
when the body hits the floor.

Ten o'clock, New England.
A local pub along a disappearing old road
somewhere near Concord.

Destruction and Creation meet in the middle,
discuss politics and religion over drinks.

They laugh, sing, cry—and promise
they won't wait so long again till their next reunion.

I have learned to hone my darkness.

I have enough darkness to fill the night sky.

I have enough light to turn the night into day.

And I have enough fire
to fill centuries of cold and loneliness
with warmth that will never fade.

He said to me about love and the world,
    "Everything is doomed!"

Doomed?
No. Everything is perishable!
Food is, humans are, the earth is,
relations of all sorts—
But just because food is going to perish,
and your body too,
doesn't mean you shouldn't eat, does it?
The same applies to love.
Love may live, and with that, may die,
but it doesn't mean you shouldn't have
chapters and passages of life
with people and the world.

The fact that everything is perishable is the
reason to live.

I went to the loveliest courthouse wedding.
My two friends kissed like they needed to.
It was like both their faces were two dimensions
opening up, their mouths,
and they were colliding,
making an even bigger sky.
My god they love each other.
When they threw the bouquet,
I dodged that shit like a bomb—
I ran, jumped, and took cover.

I can live with the fact that I was
born ignorant, have said dumb things,
and am fighting those tendencies
by learning in whatever means I can.
However, I cannot live cemented in my ways.
Never growing is the death of any living thing.
I am willing and open.

I slept through all my alarms today:

>   my radio alarm,
>   my car alarm
> & my house alarm.

When I woke up, I found myself
in the middle of a field, all those things missing,
without anything to worry about.

Charlyne Yi is a professional polymath.
She is a composer, painter, actress,
comedian, and author of *Oh the Moon*.
She currently lives on the road.